TABLE OI

MW00960590

IN THE GYM:

IN THE ROOM:

Travel isn't always pretty. It isn't always comfortable. Sometimes it hurts, it even breaks your heart. But that's okay. The journey changes you; it should change you. It leaves marks on your memory, on your consciousness, on your heart, and on your body. You take something with you. Hopefully, you leave something good behind.

~ Anthony Bourdain

HOW IT WORKS

PUT SIMPLY...

Step 1: Open it
Step 2: Read it
Step 3: Do the workouts
Step 4: Become a better version of YOU!

A LITTLE MORE DETAIL:

This is a choose your own adventure style workout book. Think of it like a set of your favorite recipes...but for your body. You can cherry pick the ones you like, you can pick ones that will challenge you, or you can bundle a few workouts together to target the areas you want to focus on.

There are two primary sections for wherever you happen to find yourself on the road. Half of the workouts are designed for a moderate level on gym equipment you may typically find in a hotel gym. The other half is for you to knock out wherever you happen to be...hotel lobby waiting to check-in, the elevator on the way to your room, or most commonly utilized...your hotel room.

We've also broken each category of workout (in the gym, or in the room) down into areas of the body you'd like to focus. Have fun and try different combinations of workouts that work different areas of the body.

The bottom line is that lack of time or equipment should never be an excuse to not get a workout in. Have fun and move that body!

ABOUT THE AUTHORS

MEET JORDAN COSTA

Ever since I was little, I've always had a passion for being active. I can directly credit my mother, Judy Walters, for this fondness for fitness. Growing up in Montana, then later Utah, and finally, Colorado, our family has always loved being active and all things outdoors.

I've carried this enthusiasm throughout every aspect of my life, from my exercise science major in College to jobs I've held, such as gym manager, CrossFit level 1 trainer, and several roles working for health and wellness companies.

As a sales professional, I've always had an extensive work travel schedule. As a result of constantly being on the road, it didn't take long for me to notice my overall commitment to getting workouts in during these trips would take a back seat to the back-to-back meetings, happy hours, and business dinners. Often crammed for time, I knew I needed to find a routine that I could follow that would allow me to still get a workout in without running late or showing up out of breath to these meetings. This is where the basis for 101 Hotel Workouts was born, and it all started with one glorious workout, affectionately dubbed 'The Jordan Special,' 100 Burpees for time.

Now living in America's finest city, San Diego, CA, I still spend as much time outdoors with my beautiful wife, Amanda and our crazy corgi, Zoe. You'll find us roaming the beaches, hiking the trails, or out on our stand up paddleboards (yes, Zoe goes on there too).

101 Hotel Workouts is now my second published book. You can find my first one, The Corgi Coloring Book, by scanning the QR code below.

ABOUT THE AUTHORS

MEET NICK SAM ADAMS

For as long as I can remember, sports were a part of my life. The oldest of five siblings, there was never a lack of competition. We found our passion on the wrestling mat, dedicated from a very young age, and heavily supported by our parents.

I learned early on the value of discipline, hard work, and the gifts that come with failure. That dedication, sometimes forced, instilled the value of simply moving my body to improve the quality of my life. I always had a consistent practice of exercise, even through the crazy college years.

Fast forward to adulthood and the stresses of daily life, work, and travel began to get me. I struggled with anxiety and depression and one of the few outlets I found relief was through pushing my body. I was fortunate to find CrossFit in my mid 30's and it offered an outlet for both a healthy lifestyle and some healthy competition. I met Jordan through this functional fitness forum and have been friends ever since.

We shared a common struggle with keeping active while on the road and traded workouts we'd concocted. We decided to write them down and share them with the world. Our mission is to eliminate all excuses for skipping the gym, no matter how busy life might get.

Today, I'm grateful to live in sunny San Diego, working in tech, building a coaching practice, and enjoying a sleepy beach lifestyle with my beautfiul partner Chelsea, and our ever growing collection of cats.

My sincere hope is that 101 Hotel Workouts provides an opportunity for anyone, no matter what shape, size, or age, to find opportunities to improve their lives through functional movement no matter where you happen to land.

ACKNOWLEDGEMENTS

JORDAN COSTA

First off, I want to thank my beautiful wife, Amanda Costa. Without her support and encouragement, this book would never have been made. She was the glue that held everything together while I was away on my work trips, and there's nobody else I'd rather be on this journey with. I love you.

Next, I want to thank my parents and brother, who have been an incredible source of inspiration for this fitness journey. We've always been an active family, and I'm so thankful that's continued into my adult life.

Finally, I want to thank my co-author Nick. Nick is an incredible life coach, and without his guidance and insistence to follow through on this idea, it would still be a blurb on the notes page on my iPhone. Thanks for the push, buddy!

NICK SAM ADAMS

Thank you, Chelsea. As a physical therapist she has taught me the value in recovery, the importance of stretching, and that no matter what, there's no excuse not to get a workout in (regardless how small). She has shown me that health and wellness is a marathon, not a sprint, and was the inspiration for a few of the workouts you will find in this book.

I'd also like to thank my parents, siblings, and every coach I've had throughout my life. I was taught the discipline of exercise and fitness at an early age. My parents were supportive through sports, my siblings offered healthy competition, and my coaches both in sports and in life have pushed me to go beyond what I thought was possible. My commitment to fitness has been the single most important aspect of my physical and mental wellbeing.

Finally, I would also like to thank my co-author, Jordan. He is infectiously positive and enriches the lives of everyone around him. He is a wealth of creativity and without his partnership, I too, would have been stuck on page 1 of this book.

Don't stop when you're tired.

Stop when you're done.

~ David Goggins

IN THE GYM

Pages 9-58 are all workouts you can do with access to a gym. We purposely designed these workouts to rely on a minimal set of equipment that any hotel or garage gym would have. While these are hotel based workouts you can do them wherever you have the right or comparable equipment and the motivation to push hard.

You can pick and choose the workouts however you'd like. Each workout targets a different set of muscle groups which is listed on each page. If you've done a significant amount of lower body and want to find some balance in the upper body, skip around however you'd like.

There is no wrong way to get these short and effective workouts done in the gym. The trip to and from may be longer than the workout itself.

I'LL NEVER LET GO

10-1 Burpee Deadlifts
1-10 Push Press

If Rose had done this workout she may have been able to hold onto Jack...and the door.

📋 DESCRIPTION:

For time, alternate movements and rep ranges. Starting at 10 and decreasing to 1 with the Burpee Deadlifts while increasing from 1 up to 10 for the Push Press.

EQUIPMENT:
Dumbbells (x2)

⏱ TIME TO COMPLETE:
For Time.

BURPEE TORNADO

100 Thrusters
5 Burpees

Don't get whisked off to Oz by getting caught in the
Burpee Tornado. Rest too long and it'll get you.

📄 DESCRIPTION:

12 minute time cap. Perform 100 thrusters in as few sets as possible while completing 5 burpees at the top of every minute.

⇤→ EQUIPMENT:

Dumbbells (x2)

⏱ TIME TO COMPLETE:

12 Minute Time Cap.

THE ELEVATORS OUT OF ORDER

1-10 Weighted Step-Ups
4 Burpees

The addition of the dumbbell for these step-ups really gives you a chance to contemplate all of your life decisions.

📋 DESCRIPTION:

For Time. After every round of step-ups complete 4 burpees, increase the reps by 1 each round, finishing at 10 step-ups.

🏋 EQUIPMENT:
Dumbbells (x1)

⏱ TIME TO COMPLETE:
For Time.

MEETING WITH HR

5 Pull-Ups
10 Push-Ups
15 Air Squats

This trio of movements is a constant theme in our book. Why? Because we're lazy and not creative... wait no that's not it, it's because they're effective. Yeah, that's it.

🖹 DESCRIPTION:

20 minutes to complete as many rounds as possible.

⊷ EQUIPMENT:

Pull-Up Bar

⏱ TIME TO COMPLETE:

20 Minute Time Cap.

IYKYK

21 Dumbbell Thrusters
21 Pull-Ups
15 Dumbbell Thrusters
15 Pull-Ups
9 Dumbbell Thrusters
9 Pull-Ups

A classic workout that will leave you breathless. Go as fast as you can.

📄 DESCRIPTION:

21 reps of both movements, then 15 reps, then finish with 9 reps of each movement for time.

◀━▶ EQUIPMENT:

Dumbbells (x2)
Pull-Up Bar

⏲ TIME TO COMPLETE:

For Time.

IHOP (NO, NOT THAT ONE)

16 Bench Hops
12 Deadlifts
 8 Strict Press

Attack this workout like a spider monkey jacked up on Mountain Dew.

📋 DESCRIPTION:

Complete 1 round of all the movements within a 2 minute window and rest the remaining time. Continue for 20 minutes (10 rounds total).

🏋 EQUIPMENT:

Bench
Dumbbells (x2)

⏱ TIME TO COMPLETE:

20 Minutes.

OVERTIME

12 Deadlifts
9 Hang Cleans
6 Push Jerks

*Can you hold onto the dumbbells the entire way
through? More importantly, should you?*

📋 DESCRIPTION:

5 rounds for time. Complete the movements in order.

🏋 EQUIPMENT:

Dumbbells (x2)

⏱ TIME TO COMPLETE:

For Time.

SPRING CLEANING

30 Clean and Jerks

The first 15 will seem like a breeze the next 15 will make you weak in the knees.

 **DESCRIPTION:**

Complete all reps for time.

 **EQUIPMENT:**

Dumbbells (x2)

TIME TO COMPLETE:

For Time.

SOMETHING WICKED THIS WAY COMES

30 Devils Press

Know the Devil you're with!

 **DESCRIPTION:**

Complete all reps for time.

 **EQUIPMENT:**

Dumbbells (x2)

⏱ TIME TO COMPLETE:

For Time.

CLOWN TEARS

50 Man Makers

What kind of sick person decided to combine a burpee, a renegade row and a thruster into one movement? Anyway, have fun.

📄 DESCRIPTION:

10 minute time cap to finish all the reps. Rest as needed but manage your pace.

⟿ EQUIPMENT:
Dumbbells (x2)

⏱ TIME TO COMPLETE:
10 Minute Time Cap.

AIRPORT SHUTTLE

10 Shuttle Sprints (25 Feet)
10 Dumbbell Squats
10 Plank Rows
10 Shoot Throughs

*In ancient Mayan and Aztec times, 10 was believed
to be the end and the beginning of the cycle, bringing
both death, and new life. Seems appropriate for
this workout.*

🗒 DESCRIPTION:

Complete 10 rounds for time.

 ## EQUIPMENT:

Dumbbells (x2)

⏱ TIME TO COMPLETE:

For Time.

40'S THE NEW 30

400 Meter Treadmill Run (.25 mi)
40 Push-Ups
40 Superman's
40 Air Squats
5 Minute Rest
40 Burpee Cash Out

4 rounds to earn that networking dinner you have later tonight but the burpees are where you earn your dessert.

📋 DESCRIPTION:

Complete 4 rounds including the rest and the Burpee cash out within a 40 minute time cap.

🏋 EQUIPMENT:
Treadmill

⏱ TIME TO COMPLETE:
40 Minute Time Cap.

PLEASE DON'T HATE US!

50 Burpees
400 Meter Treadmill Run (.25 mi)
100 Push-Ups
400 Meter Treadmill Run (.25 mi)
150 Walking Lunges
400 Meter Treadmill Run (.25 mi)
200 Air Squats
400 Meter Treadmill Run (.25 mi)
150 Walking Lunges
400 Meter Treadmill Run (.25 mi)
100 Push-Ups
400 Meter Treadmill Run (.25 mi)
50 Burpees

No clock will save you here. This is a long chipper style workout that will remind you that nothing is given and everything is earned.

🗒 DESCRIPTION:

For Time. Complete the whole movement before moving onto the next one.

⬌ EQUIPMENT:

Treadmill

⏱ TIME TO COMPLETE:

For Time.

BURPEE SANDWICH

10 Burpees
20 Dumbbell Snatch
30 Dumbbell Push Press
40 Overhead Lunges
30 Dumbbell Push Press
20 Dumbbell Snatch
10 Burpees

One dumbbell and a whole lot of fun. Make sure to alternate arms as you see fit to save your grip. All you have to do is go up and down the ladder.

📋 DESCRIPTION:

For time. Complete the whole movement before moving onto the next one.

 EQUIPMENT:

Dumbbells (x1)

⏱ TIME TO COMPLETE:

For Time.

JET LAG

200 Meter Treadmill Run
20 Jump Squats
10 Burpees
10 Hand Release Push-Ups

This works out to 3 minutes per round if you want to finish, push on the gas the whole time. You're a rockstar if you can finish in 10 minutes. You're still the lead guitar player even if you don't.

DESCRIPTION:

5 Rounds with a 15 minute time cap.

EQUIPMENT:

Treadmill

TIME TO COMPLETE:

15 Minute Time Cap.

FROM 6 TO MIDNIGHT

6-9-12
Hang Clean and Jerk (right arm)
Dumbbell Overhead Squat
Hang Clean and Jerk (left arm)
Dumbbell Overhead Squat

It's 5 O'clock somewhere, so you better get moving.

📄 DESCRIPTION:

5 minute time cap to complete. Complete 6 reps of each movement, then 9 reps, then 12 reps in ascending order.

🏋 EQUIPMENT:

Dumbbells (x1)

⏱ TIME TO COMPLETE:

5 Minute Time Cap.

GOING PUBLIC

8 Dumbbell Hops
10 Dumbbell Toe Taps
12 Plank Dumbbell Cross-Body Touches
14 Dumbbell Leg Lifts

You might need a calculus degree to keep all these numbers straight but what you won't need are any eggs because you'll be yoked!

📄 DESCRIPTION:

Complete 4 reps each side of the dumbbell hops, 5 reps each side of the dumbbell toe taps, 6 reps each side of the plank dumbbell cross-body touches, and 7 reps each side of the dumbbell leg lifts. As many rounds as possible in 12 minutes.

⟺ EQUIPMENT:
Dumbbells (x1)

⏱ TIME TO COMPLETE:
12 Minute Time Cap.

NICK & JORDAN ARE JERKS

100 Burpees Over Dumbbell

*Just because it's simple, doesn't mean it's easy.
Challenge accepted.*

📋 DESCRIPTION:

Perform 100 dumbbell facing burpees for time.

🏋 EQUIPMENT:

Dumbbells (x1)

⏱ TIME TO COMPLETE:

For Time.

BRING A FRIEND TO WORK DAY

Treadmill Dumbbell Walk

Dumbbells don't have legs (duh) but they still like to see the sights. That's where you come in. Take your new buddy for a walk but don't drop him, that makes him and everyone around you sad.

🗒 DESCRIPTION:

Max distance for time. Just continue walking with a single dumbbell in hand. You can switch hands as needed or change position but you cannot put the dumbbell down.

EQUIPMENT:
Dumbbells (x1)

⏱ TIME TO COMPLETE:
For Time.

ANNUAL REVIEW

400m Treadmill Run
25 Pull-Ups
50 Push-Ups
75 Air Squats

If dinner is at 7 pm and you start this at 6 pm, we're confident you'll make it there before the appetizers arrive.

DESCRIPTION:

Complete 4 rounds for time. Take breaks as needed early so the later sets are easier to manage.

 **EQUIPMENT:**
Treadmill
Pull-Up Bar
Body Weight

⏱ TIME TO COMPLETE:
For Time.

TAKING A TRIP TO PITY CITY

10-1 Hang Dumbbell Squat Clean
1-10 Burpees Over The Dumbbells

One of our favorite rep schemes. Delightfully grueling on both ends. Have fun.

📄 DESCRIPTION:

10 total rounds. Round 1 begins with 10 hang dumbbell squat cleans and 1 burpee over dumbbells, round 2 is 9 hang dumbbell squat cleans and 2 burpees. Continue until you complete all 10 rounds for time.

🏋 EQUIPMENT:
Dumbbells (x2)

⏱ TIME TO COMPLETE:
For Time.

STOP AND SMELL THE CARPET

1 mile Treadmill Run
10 Push-Ups

The faster you run the less push-ups you have to do.
#science

📄 DESCRIPTION:

1 mile for time. Every minute stop and perform 10 push-ups.

🏋 EQUIPMENT:

Treadmill
Body weight

⏱ TIME TO COMPLETE:

For Time.

WORKING ON THE WEEKEND

20 Renegade Rows
15 Dumbbell Deadlift
10 Dumbbell Strict Press

Warning. This workout may cause an increase in self confidence, compliments, and compulsive desire to say things like, 'gainz' and 'swole'.

📄 DESCRIPTION:
Complete 4 rounds for time.

EQUIPMENT:
Dumbbells (x2)

⏱ TIME TO COMPLETE:
For Time.

JUMPING JERKS

30 Jumping Lunges
5 Dumbbell Hang Clean and Jerks

150 total jumping lunges in this workout.
Enough said.

 **DESCRIPTION:**
5 total rounds for time.

EQUIPMENT:
Dumbbells (x2)

TIME TO COMPLETE:
For Time.

WORKING 9 TO 5

9 Dumbbell Thrusters
8 Sprawls
7 Dumbbell Deadlifts
6 Push-Ups
5 Dumbbell Hang Cleans

Don't let the Sunday scaries get you on this one. At least this workout isn't as bad as the commute home in rush hour traffic.

DESCRIPTION:
Complete 5 rounds for time.

 **EQUIPMENT:**
Dumbbells (x2)

TIME TO COMPLETE:
For Time.

INTERNATIONAL TRAVEL

10 Bulgarian Split Squats
10 Russian Twists
10 Single-Leg Romanian Deadlifts
5 Turkish Get-Ups

* All reps are on each side

We could go with a side of French fries to compliment this workout.

 DESCRIPTION:
Complete 3 rounds for time.

EQUIPMENT:
Dumbbells (x1)

TIME TO COMPLETE:
For Time.

HALL PASS

Walk in, look around, then leave.

*You can honestly say you went to the gym today
(but we secretly think once you get there, you'll do
something).*

📋 DESCRIPTION:
Walk in, look around, then leave.

 EQUIPMENT:
Body Weight

⏱ TIME TO COMPLETE:
For Time.

TSA PRECHECK

50 Clusters

The cluster is nothing more than the unholy union of the clean and a thruster.

📄 DESCRIPTION:

Complete 50 reps for time.

🏋 EQUIPMENT:
Dumbbells (x2)

⏱ TIME TO COMPLETE:
For Time.

RETIREMENT PARTY

Jumping Air Squats
Dumbbell Sumo Deadlift High Pulls
Bench Step Ups
Push Press
Treadmill Run
Rest

* 1 minute each movement

No gold Rolex for finishing this workout but you'll have earned plenty of sweat equity.

📄 DESCRIPTION:

Complete 1 minute of each movement including a minute of rest. Complete 3 total rounds for max reps.

⟜ EQUIPMENT:
Dumbbells (x2)
Bench
Treadmill

⏱ TIME TO COMPLETE:
EMOM x 3 Rounds.

CLIMB THE CORPORATE LADDER

5 Deadlifts
5 Squats
5 Bicep Curls
5 Shoulder Press

The only way to get to the top is one rung at a time.

📄 DESCRIPTION:

Complete 5 total rounds for time. Push yourself but focus on your form. Isolate the movements and muscle groups throughout.

🏋 EQUIPMENT:

Dumbbells (x2)

⏱ TIME TO COMPLETE:

For Time.

HOSTILE TAKEOVER

5 Deadlift
5 Hang Power Clean
5 Front Squat
5 Push Press

*Bonus points and a high five if you hold onto the
dumbbells for all 5 rounds. Why not add forearms to
the rest of the body's burn?*

DESCRIPTION:

Complete 5 total rounds of each movement for time.

EQUIPMENT:
Dumbbells (x2)

TIME TO COMPLETE:
For Time.

THE COCKY BOSS

100 Bench Press

Get this done in as few sets as possible. The faster you do it, the faster you're done.

 **DESCRIPTION:**

Finish all of the reps in 10 minutes or less.

EQUIPMENT:

Dumbbells (x2)

TIME TO COMPLETE:

For Time.

TAKE 5

20 Burpees
20 Pull-Ups
20 Dips
20 Push-Ups
20 Sit-Ups

The perfect workout for when you just arrived at the
hotel and only have 10 minutes until Happy Hour.

📄 DESCRIPTION:

5 minute time cap to complete all the movements in order.

🏋 EQUIPMENT:
Pull-Up Bar
Bench

⏱ TIME TO COMPLETE:
5 Minute Time Cap.

JUST HANGING OUT

2 Farmers Carry (Gym)
1 Min Dead Hang from Pull-Up Bar
2 Farmers Carry (Gym)

*Pro Tip: Go as heavy on the dumbbells as possible
If you can not hold the entire minute hanging from
the pull-up bar, it's okay to drop and accumulate a
minute total.*

📄 DESCRIPTION:

3 Rounds for time. Go 2 lengths of the gym for both farmer's
carry.

⇤⇥ EQUIPMENT:
Dumbbells (x2)

⏱ TIME TO COMPLETE:
For Time.

BEAR TO BULL MARKET

10 Deficit Push-Ups (right arm on DB)

20 Mountain Climbers

10 Deficit Push-Ups (left arm on DB)

20 Mountain Climbers

Invest your pace wisely. Invest too much early on and this thing will be a bear. Too slow and you'll be bullying your way through traffic to make dinner on time.

 DESCRIPTION:
Complete 4 rounds for time.

EQUIPMENT:
Dumbbells (x1)

⏱ TIME TO COMPLETE:
For Time.

QUARTERLY EARNINGS

400 Meter Treadmill Run (.25 mi)
15 Overhead Squats

1 meter = 0.0006213712 miles. Bet you didn't expect to get a mental workout as well. You're welcome!

 **DESCRIPTION:**
5 rounds for time.

 **EQUIPMENT:**
Treadmill
Dumbbells (x1)

 **TIME TO COMPLETE:**
For Time.

LETS CIRCLE BACK

100 Meter Jog Forward
100 Meter Shuffle Step to the left
100 Meter Jog Backward
100 Meter Shuffle Step to the right

You'll get a full 360 degree view of the gym with this
one. This may push personal space to a new level.

📋 DESCRIPTION:

4 rounds for time. This will accumulate 1 mile in total distance.

🏋 EQUIPMENT:
Treadmill

⏱ TIME TO COMPLETE:
For Time.

CLIMBING EVEREST SOLO

Dumbbell Back Squats (max set)

Technically 1 rep counts as an unbroken set and a workout (hey we're not here to judge) but we'd recommend going for at least 50 reps. This one is between you, and you.

📋 DESCRIPTION:
Pick a weight you can move with. Once you start you don't stop until failure.

🏋 EQUIPMENT:
Dumbbells (x2)

⏱ TIME TO COMPLETE:
Max Reps.

CORGI BUTT

12 Sumo Deadlifts
12 Lateral Lunges
12 Reverse Lunges
12 Weighted Squat jumps

Aren't Corgi butt's the best! Like seriously, they are so freaking cute, we can't even. Anyway, here's a booty burner for you.

📄 DESCRIPTION:

As many rounds as possible in 15 minutes.

 EQUIPMENT:

Dumbbells (x1)

⏱ TIME TO COMPLETE:

15 Minute Time Cap.

MOVING ROCKS

30 Russian Twists
20 Weighted Lunges
10 Snatches

This core workout produces a full body sweat. Hope you brought a change of clothes.

📄 DESCRIPTION:

5 rounds for time. Use 1 dumbbell for all of the movements.

🏋 EQUIPMENT:

Dumbbells (x1)

⏱ TIME TO COMPLETE:

For Time.

ROOM SERVICE

30 Snatches
20 Hanging Knee Raises

Step 1. Order room service.
Step 2. Run down to the gym and finish this workout.
Step 3. Make it back before your meal arrives and enjoy.

📄 DESCRIPTION:
5 minute time cap to complete both movements.

🏋 EQUIPMENT:
Dumbbells (x1)
Pull-Up bar

⏱ TIME TO COMPLETE:
5 Minute Time Cap.

PLANKS FOR NOTHING

20 Wall Balls
1 Minute Plank

These planks make the last 2 rounds of wall balls extra spicy!

 **DESCRIPTION:**

Complete 5 rounds for time.

EQUIPMENT:

Medicine Ball

TIME TO COMPLETE:

For Time.

CORE PRINCIPLES

800 Meter Treadmill Run (.5 mi)
60 V-Ups
800 Meter Treadmill Run (.5 mi)
75 Tuck-Ups
800 Meter Treadmill Run (.5 mi)
90 Mountain Climbers

Legs and abs, abs and legs, what more could you ask for?

📋 DESCRIPTION:
For Time. Complete the whole movement before moving onto the next one.

🏋 EQUIPMENT:
Treadmill

⏱ TIME TO COMPLETE:
For Time.

RUNNING ERRANDS

5K Treadmill Run (3.1 mi)

It doesn't have to be complicated to be effective.

📄 DESCRIPTION:
Complete a 5K run for time.

 EQUIPMENT:
Treadmill

⏱ TIME TO COMPLETE:
For Time.

2 MINUTE WARNING

30 Minute Treadmill Run
10 Burpees (every 2 minutes)

Is the run a rest from the burpees or are the burpees
a rest from the run? Something to contemplate for the
next 30 minutes.

📄 DESCRIPTION:
30 minutes to complete max distance on the treadmill stopping
every 2 minutes to perform 10 burpees.

🏋 EQUIPMENT:
Treadmill

⏱ TIME TO COMPLETE:
30 Minutes.

WHY THOUGH?

100 Back Squats
5 Burpees

The faster you go, the fewer burpees you'll have to do. That's just solid math.

📄 DESCRIPTION:

For time, complete 100 back squats in as few sets as possible while stopping every minute to perform 5 burpees over the dumbbell.

🏋 EQUIPMENT:
Dumbbells (x2)

⏱ TIME TO COMPLETE:
For Time.

1 MINUTE IS LONG ENOUGH

Dumbbell Bear Crawl (Gym)
10 Deadlifts
Dumbbell Walking Lunges (Gym)
10 Deadlifts
Rest 1 Min

Pick a weight that you can hold onto the whole time.
You'll have a minute between rounds to rest your grip
so hold on.

📋 DESCRIPTION:

10 rounds for time. Rest 1 minute in between rounds. Do 1 gym
length distance for dumbbell bear crawls and dumbbell walking
Lunges.

⟐ EQUIPMENT:
Dumbbells (x2)

⏱ TIME TO COMPLETE:
For Time.

ROWING UP A MOUNTAIN

1-10
Renegade Rows (each side)
Push-Ups
Mountain Climbers

Only 1 rep each, that's it? As if we'd be that nice. Add
1 rep each round, finishing at 10 reps. Sorry not sorry.

📋 DESCRIPTION:

10 rounds total, after the first round of 1 rep for each movement
add 1 additional rep each round.

🏋 EQUIPMENT:
Dumbbells (x2)

⏱ TIME TO COMPLETE:
For Time.

STUCK IN THE MIDDLE SEAT

20 Russian Twists
15 Pullovers
10 Chest Press (each side)

Twist, pull, press. Reminds us of that game Bop It.
Anyone remember that? This is way more fun.

📄 DESCRIPTION:

Complete each movement every minute on the minute. Minute
1 complete 20 russian twists, minute 2 complete 15 pullovers,
minute 3 complete 10 chest press (each side). Then start back at
the top.

🏋 EQUIPMENT:
Dumbbells (x1)

⏱ TIME TO COMPLETE:
15 Minute EMOM.

ASKING FOR A RAISE

50 Burpee Pull-Ups

We've yet again found another way to make burpees even worse. Seems to be a running theme.

 DESCRIPTION:

Complete 50 burpee pull-ups for time.

EQUIPMENT:

Pull-Up Bar

⏱ TIME TO COMPLETE:

For Time.

The more you seek the uncomfortable, the more you will become comfortable.

~ Conor McGregor

IN THE ROOM

The remainder of the workouts in this book are those you can do with only what you traveled with or nothing at all. All excuses (including time) are elimintated from the workouts that follow.

Whether you have just 5 minutes or 50, you can find a workout that gets your body feeling good and your head in the right place. Our intention was to create workouts that can be done by a beginner but can be pushed by anyone further along their fitness journey.

Just like the first half of the book, you can pick and choose the workouts however you'd like. Each workout targets a different set of muscle groups which is listed in the table of contents. If you've done a significant amount of lower body and want to find some balance in the upper body, just look through and find ones that meet your needs.

There is no wrong way to get these short and effective workouts done in the hotel room before that big meeting, casual happy hour, or a long day of conference attendance.

You are on your way to a happy and healthier life.

THE JORDAN SPECIAL

100 Burpees

The original workout that inspired this book.

 **DESCRIPTION:**

Perform 100 burpees for time.

EQUIPMENT:

Body Weight

TIME TO COMPLETE:

For Time.

SWEAT DOWN THE LADDER

10-1 Push-Up
10-1 Air Squat
10-1 Sit-Up

So simple, so effective, so sweaty.

📄 DESCRIPTION:

Perform each movement starting with 10 reps. Once completed
perform each movement again for 9 reps and so on down until
you've reached 1 rep of each.

🏋 EQUIPMENT:
Body Weight

⏱ TIME TO COMPLETE:
For Time.

100%

100 Push-Up
100 Air Squat
100 Sit-Up

This one gets spicy quickly. Feel the pump and avoid too large of a first set.

📄 DESCRIPTION:

Perform 100 reps of each movement. Partition however you'd like (ex 25 reps each for 4 rounds).

⟷ EQUIPMENT:
Body Weight

⏱ TIME TO COMPLETE:
For Time.

NO INCIDENTALS

100 Wall Balls

* 1 minute plank each time you rest

No walls were harmed in the making of this workout.

📋 DESCRIPTION:

Complete 100 wall balls for time. Everytime you break to rest perform a 1 minute plank.

EQUIPMENT:
Backpack or Pillow

⏱ TIME TO COMPLETE:
For Time.

CINDY WANTS ABS

5 Push-Ups
10 Air Squats
15 Sit-Ups

Set a pace and stick to it. Too fast off the gun and you'll turn this from a 20 minute sweat session to a 20 minute prison sentence.

📋 DESCRIPTION:

As many rounds as possible in 20 minutes.

🏋 EQUIPMENT:
Body Weight

⏱ TIME TO COMPLETE:
20 Minute Time Cap.

BURNING THE MIDNIGHT OIL

10 Burpees
20 Jumping Jacks
30 Squats
40 Push-Ups
50 Lunges (25 on each side)

*Burn those legs and watch the ceiling. We're doing
some jumping 'round the room today.*

🗒 DESCRIPTION:

As many rounds as possible in 20 minutes.

⊷ EQUIPMENT:

Body Weight

⏱ TIME TO COMPLETE:

20 Minute Time Cap.

CONNECTING FLIGHTS

50 Burpees
1 Minute Run In Place
100 Push-Ups
1 Minute Run In Place
150 Walking Lunges
1 Minute Run In Place
200 Squats
1 Minute Run In Place
150 Walking Lunges
1 Minute Run In Place
100 Push-Ups
1 Minute Run In Place
50 Burpees

It's like eating an elephant. One bite at a time.

📄 DESCRIPTION:

Chipper style. Start at the top and work your way down the list. Take break as needed and don't burn out too early.

🏋 EQUIPMENT:
Body Weight

⏱ TIME TO COMPLETE:
For Time.

TRAIN HOPPING

Lateral Hop Over Suitcase and Back
1 Push-Up
4 Lateral Hop Over Suitcase
2 Push-Ups
4 Lateral Hop Over Suitcase
3 Push-Ups

This workout won't just work the calves but will teach you to pack a smaller bag in the future.

📄 DESCRIPTION:

The suitcase hop overs stay the same every round. Push-ups start with 1 and you add a rep each round until you finish the round of 10 Push-Ups.

🏋 EQUIPMENT:
Body Weight
Suitcase

⏱ TIME TO COMPLETE:
For Time.

SPRAWL TILL YOU FALL

1 Suitcase Sprawl
1 Suitcase Clean and Press

*The clean and press will be what slows you down
here and that all depends on how much you 'unpack'
your suitcase.*

📄 DESCRIPTION:

Alternating movements. Perform 30 reps total of each exercise
for time.

🏋 EQUIPMENT:

Body Weight
Suitcase

⏱ TIME TO COMPLETE:

For Time.

BREAK IN CASE OF EMERGENCY

1 Wall Sit
10 Push-Ups
10 Sit-Ups

A little spice thrown into the wall sit soup.

📋 DESCRIPTION:

Accumulate 10 total minutes. Every time you break perform 10 push-ups and 10 sit-ups.

🏋 EQUIPMENT:

Body Weight

⏱ TIME TO COMPLETE:

10 Total Minutes.

JUST THE TIPPY TOES

20 Toe Taps
10 Sprawls

Two great movements guaranteed to get your heart rate up and keep it there. Perhaps we should combine both movements into one fun name. Trawls? Spraps? Those are both awful. Anyway, have fun.

 DESCRIPTION:

5 total rounds. Using your suitcase as a point of contact, quickly tap the top of your suitcase with your foot alternating legs then move onto the sprawls.

EQUIPMENT:
Body Weight
Suitcase

TIME TO COMPLETE:
For Time.

THE 300

10 Squats
10 Handstand Shoulder Taps
20 Squats
20 Handstand Shoulder Taps
30 Squats
30 Handstand Shoulder Taps
40 Squats
40 Handstand Shoulder Taps
50 Squats
50 Handstand Shoulder Taps

The handstand shoulder tap may be one of our most complicated movements. So why not make you do 150 of them. You're welcome.

📄 DESCRIPTION:

In descending order work your way down completing each movement along the way. Work to your ability for the handstand shoulder taps.

🏋 EQUIPMENT:
Body Weight

⏱ TIME TO COMPLETE:
For Time.

R.I.P. (RUNNING IN PLACE)

1 Minute Run in place
20 Jump Squats
10 Burpees
10 Hand release Push-Ups

Another one to make sure your downstairs neighbor makes their early morning meeting on time.

 **DESCRIPTION:**
5 rounds for time, alternating movements.

EQUIPMENT:
Body Weight

TIME TO COMPLETE:
For Time.

TABATA YOU TALKING ABOUT?

Push-Ups
Sit-Ups
High Knees
Jumping Lunges

* Alternating movements

Tabata
[tə bädə]
NOUN
a form of high-intensity physical training in which
very short periods of extremely demanding activity
are alternated with shorter periods of rest.

📑 DESCRIPTION:

Tabata style. :20 seconds of work, :10 seconds of rest for 4 total rounds (8 minutes total).

◀━▶ EQUIPMENT:
Body Weight

⏱ TIME TO COMPLETE:
8 Minutes.

WALKING IN CIRCLES

4 Room Lengths - Single Arm Farmers Carry (right arm)
12 Deadlifts
4 Room Lengths - Single Arm Farmers Carry (left arm)
12 Deadlifts

You may wish you hadn't upgraded to the suite for this one.

📄 DESCRIPTION:
4 rounds for time. Alternating arms each round.

🏋 EQUIPMENT:
Suitcase

⏱ TIME TO COMPLETE:
For Time.

THE INVERTED TURTLE

100 Floor Press
50 Flutter kicks

Imagine an upside down turtle doing a bench press. If that visual makes you giggle, don't worry, the flutter kicks will end that quickly.

📄 DESCRIPTION:

Lying on your back holding your suitcase or chair, press it towards the ceiling. Try to complete 100 reps in as few sets as possible. Every time you break, set the suitcase/chair to the side and perform 50 flutter kicks before starting again.

🏋 EQUIPMENT:

Suitcase
Chair

⏱ TIME TO COMPLETE:

For Time.

READY FOR TAKEOFF

50-40-30-20-10

Jump Rope
Sit-Ups

The only thing harder than jump roping is pretending to jump rope!

📄 DESCRIPTION:

Both movements have the same number of reps. Start at the top and work your way down. For the 'jump ropes' you can use two washcloths or two t-shirts. The goal is to add a bit of weight in your hands and help to simulate the 'jump rope' motions.

⫟ EQUIPMENT:
Small Towels or Shirts
Body Weight

⏱ TIME TO COMPLETE:
For Time.

CHAIRMAN OF THE BOARD

7 Dips on Chair
7 Steps Ups on Chair
7 Push-Ups on Chair

Would not advise doing this on a rocking chair.

📄 DESCRIPTION:

Complete 7 rounds for time. For the push-ups on the chair, position yourself in an inclined plank with feet on the floor and hands on the chair. For the dips, keep your back towards the seat of the chair with your hands on the edge. Straighten your legs to make it more difficult or put a slight bend in your knees to make it easier.

〰 EQUIPMENT:

Body Weight
Chair

⏱ TIME TO COMPLETE:

For Time.

THIS MEETING COULD'VE BEEN AN EMAIL

EMOM for 20 Minutes

1 Minute Lunges
1 Minute Push-Ups
1 Minute Jump Squats
1 Minute Suitcase High Pulls

How much work will you put in during these high pulls? Well, Work = Force x Distance, soooooo you do the math.

📋 DESCRIPTION:

20 minute EMOM (every minute on the minute). Each minute work on one movement attempting as many reps as you can get in that minute before moving on to the next movement/minute.

🏋 EQUIPMENT:
Body Weight

⏱ TIME TO COMPLETE:
20 Minutes.

THE TRIFECTA

100 Hand Release Push-Ups
100 Straight Leg Sit-Ups
100 Jumping Air Squats

Taking 3 fundamental movements and in true Nick &
Jordan fashion - we've made it harder. If you've made
quick work of 100% on page 63 then this should be
your next challenge.

📋 DESCRIPTION:

Complete 1 movement before moving to the next. You can
partition as needed but either way you have 300 reps to get
through.

🏋 EQUIPMENT:
Body Weight

⏱ TIME TO COMPLETE:
For Time.

DINNER IN 5

21-15-9

Air Squats
Push-Ups

When you only have 3 minutes to spare, let this be
your go-to. It's meant to be done quick, fast, and
in a hurry.

📄 DESCRIPTION:

Complete both movements for 21 reps of each, then for 15 reps
of each, then for 9 reps of each.

⟷ EQUIPMENT:
Body Weight

⏱ TIME TO COMPLETE:
For Time.

SIGHTSEEING

10 Walking Lunges
10 Push-Ups

Walking and pushing. Sounds like us whenever we're trying to get to those Costco samples, sorry not sorry, they're free and delicious.

 DESCRIPTION:

Complete each round of alternating movements for 10 total rounds. For Time.

EQUIPMENT:
Body Weight

TIME TO COMPLETE:
For Time.

1,000 REPS

100 Jumping Jacks
100 Mountain Climbers

Sounds simple enough right (insert evil laugh here)?

 DESCRIPTION:

Complete 5 total rounds of both movements for time.

EQUIPMENT:
Body Weight

TIME TO COMPLETE:
For Time.

TOP HEAVY

Dips
Push-ups

* Alternating Tabata (0:20 seconds of work 0:10 seconds of rest)

You might need to move up a shirt size after this upper body pump sesh!

📋 DESCRIPTION:
Alternating movements. 0:20 seconds of work, 0:10 seconds of rest for 8 minutes total.

⬌ EQUIPMENT:
Chair or side of the bed

⏱ TIME TO COMPLETE:
8 Minutes Total.

LET ME CARRY YOUR LUGGAGE

7 Suitcase Bicep curls (bottom to 90 degrees)

7 Suitcase bicep curls (top to 90 degrees)

7 Suitcase bicep curls (full range of motion)

We added one extra rep so you don't unintentionally summon any demons with a 6/6/6 rep scheme.

DESCRIPTION:

3 rounds total (21 reps each round). First set of 7 is from the bottom to the 90 degrees, second set of 7 is from the top of the curl to 90 degrees, and the final set of 7 is full motion from bottom to top.

EQUIPMENT:
Body Weight
Suitcase

TIME TO COMPLETE:
For Time.

PRE DINNER PUMP

1 Suitcase Bicep Curl
1 Strict Press
1 Behind the Neck Tricep Extension

Rest before you need to, this one goes uphill fast.

📄 DESCRIPTION:

Perform all 3 movements to equal 1 rep. Complete 10 reps to equal 1 round. Perform 5 rounds total.

🏋 EQUIPMENT:

Body Weight
Suitcase

⏱ TIME TO COMPLETE:

For Time.

PUSH-UP 21'S

7 Push-Ups with hands on the bed
7 standard Push-Ups on the floor
7 Push-Ups with your feet on the bed

You know what they say...the bigger the chest, the smaller the belly.

📄 DESCRIPTION:
3 total sets (21 reps per set).

🏋 EQUIPMENT:
Body Weight
Bed

⏱ TIME TO COMPLETE:
For Time.

THE DEAL CLOSER

Door Hold (right hand)
Door Hold (left hand)

This will develop a power handshake that can close any deal.

📄 DESCRIPTION:

Tabata style. :20 seconds of work, :10 seconds of rest for 8 total rounds (4 minutes total). With alternating hands, grip the bathroom door and lean back to a challenging angle (with a slight bend in your knees). Make sure you feel tension in your hand, forearm, and lats. Hold this position alternating hands every :30 seconds.

🏋 EQUIPMENT:
Body Weight

⏱ TIME TO COMPLETE:
4 Minutes.

JORDAN'S FAVORITE

100 Push-Ups

Fun Fact: Every December we have a challenge where we do this daily. Feel free to join us!

📄 DESCRIPTION:

Complete 100 total push-ups for time. Rest as needed.

 **EQUIPMENT:**
Body Weight

⏱ TIME TO COMPLETE:
For Time.

PACK LIGHT

100 Overhead Lunges

The question here is, do you leave the suitcase packed or not? There is no wrong answer.

📄 DESCRIPTION:

Lift your suitcase over your head and complete the 100 reps in as few sets as possible.

🏋 EQUIPMENT:
Suitcase

⏱ TIME TO COMPLETE:
For Time.

OH, QUAD DAMN!

10 Alternating Pistols
15 Air Squats
20 Burpees

Who brought the pistol to the party?

🗎 DESCRIPTION:

5 rounds for time. Go as low as comfortable on the pistols. Use the edge of the bed if needed.

◄—► EQUIPMENT:
Body Weight

⌚ TIME TO COMPLETE:
For Time.

TABLE FOR ONE

Wall Sit

* Accumulate 10 total minutes

Suck it up and go somewhere else for a bit.

📄 DESCRIPTION:

Don't burn yourself out early. Pick a timeframe and stick to it. Take breaks as needed.

🏋 EQUIPMENT:
Body Weight

⏱ TIME TO COMPLETE:
10 Total Minutes.

BE THE FLAMINGO

1 Single Leg Wall Sit

* Accumulate 5 total minutes

Channel your inner flamingo.

📋 DESCRIPTION:
Accumulate 5 minutes alternating legs every 0:30 seconds.

🏋 EQUIPMENT:
Body Weight

⏱ TIME TO COMPLETE:
5 Total Minutes.

PLIES > PIES

100 Plie Squats

Some may say you're bow legged. We like to think you're the definition of a rugged cowboy (or cowgirl)!

📄 DESCRIPTION:

Turn your toes out to the side (45 degrees). Your feet should be wider than shoulder-width apart. Lower yourself into a squat position. Then stand straight up. Complete 100 reps for time.

🏋 EQUIPMENT:

Body Weight

⏱ TIME TO COMPLETE:

For Time.

HOLD PLEASE

20 Jumping Lunges (alternating legs)
10 Jumping Air Squats
:30 Second Squat Hold

*Have you ever heard of Bambi legs? When you try to
walk down to the bar after this one, you'll know
what we mean.*

 **DESCRIPTION:**

Complete all 3 movements to equal 1 round. 5 total rounds
for time.

EQUIPMENT:
Body Weight

TIME TO COMPLETE:
For Time.

MEET THE NEIGHBORS

8 Suitcase Hops (clockwise)
8 Suitcase Hops (counterclockwise)

This workout creates a great opportunity to have an impromptu meet and greet with your fellow travelers staying below you.

📋 DESCRIPTION:

4 total rounds. Starting on any corner of your suitcase hop clockwise to the next corner and continue until you've hopped to each corner twice, then reverse direction and do the same thing. Rest as needed.

🏋 EQUIPMENT:
Body Weight
Suitcase

⏱ TIME TO COMPLETE:
For Time.

HOLD STILL

Weighted Wall Sit Hold

* Accumulate 5 total minutes

Hold onto that suitcase like it was a winning lottery ticket.

 **DESCRIPTION:**

Holding onto your suitcase, lean against a wall into a wall sit hold and utilize the weight of the suitcase to make it more difficult. Accumulate 5 minutes total, breaking as needed.

EQUIPMENT:
Suitcase

TIME TO COMPLETE:
5 Accumulated Minutes.

HAPPY TRAILS

1 Room Length Side Lunge (right side)
1 Room Length High knee
1 Room Length Side Lunge (left side)
1 Room Length High knee

10 minutes for you and your room to become well acquainted. Be the Roomba!.

📋 DESCRIPTION:

Perform each movement for 1 room length apiece. As many rounds as possible in 10 minutes is the goal.

🏋 EQUIPMENT:

Body Weight

⏱ TIME TO COMPLETE:

10 Minutes.

ZERO GRAVITY

200 Air Squats

Can you go unbroken? Should you? The answer is always yes.

📋 DESCRIPTION:

Pretty straight and to the point. Perform 200 air squats for time.

🏋 EQUIPMENT:
Body Weight

⏱ TIME TO COMPLETE:
For Time.

CAN'T SPELL LEGENDARY WITHOUT LEG DAY

30 Jumping Jacks
30 Burpees
30 Air Squats

Did you ever wonder who Jack was and why he was always jumping? We sure do.

 DESCRIPTION:

Complete 3 total rounds for time.

⚖ EQUIPMENT:

Body Weight

⏱ TIME TO COMPLETE:

For Time.

FREQUENT FLYER MILES

25 Jumping Squats

Just enough that you might want to take the elevator after.

 **DESCRIPTION:**

Pretty straightforward. Complete 4 rounds of 25 reps for time. Rest as needed in between rounds.

 **EQUIPMENT:**
Body Weight

⏱ **TIME TO COMPLETE:**
For Time.

POSTERIOR CHAIN-REACTION

10 Lying Hip Raises (glute bridges)
10 Donkey Kicks
10 Fire Hydrant

Sometimes fitness gets funky. Channel your inner jackass.

📋 DESCRIPTION:
3 rounds for time, alternating legs and movements.

🏋 EQUIPMENT:
Body Weight

⏱ TIME TO COMPLETE:
For Time.

SPEED FITNESS

20 Single Leg V-Ups
20 Sit-Ups
20 Side Crunches

Cash Out: 5 Minute Plank

*15 minute time cap including the 5 min plank. We're
no mathematician but our calculations show that you
better be moving to get through that first part!*

📄 DESCRIPTION:

Complete 5 total rounds. After all 5 rounds finish with a 5 min
accumulated total plank. Take breaks as needed but must
accumulate 5 total minutes to finish.

 EQUIPMENT:

Body Weight

⏱ TIME TO COMPLETE:

15 Minute Time Cap.

UNPACK A SIX PACK

1 Suitcase static press
1 Lying leg raises

Be the oil derrick. Challenge yourself by limiting the time your legs rest on the floor.

📄 DESCRIPTION:

Lying on your back with the suitcase pressed toward the ceiling, raise your straight legs and try to touch the suitcase before bringing them back to the floor. Go until you can't hold the suitcase anymore. Ideally, keep your legs straight.

🏋 EQUIPMENT:

Body Weight
Suitcase

⏱ TIME TO COMPLETE:

For Time.

CORE VALUES

1 Minute Flutter Kicks
1 Minute Wall Walks
1 Minute Crunches
1 Minute Burpees
1 Minute V-Ups

Walking on the floor is so last year. Walking on the walls, now that's where it's at!

📄 DESCRIPTION:

1 minute for each movement from top to bottom. Complete 2 total rounds.

🏋 EQUIPMENT:

Body Weight

⏱ TIME TO COMPLETE:

10 Minutes.

WHOLE LOTTA NO REST

Lunges
Plank Holds

* Alternating Tabata (0:20 seconds of work 0:10 seconds of rest)

Keep your eyes on the clock here, 0:20 seconds of work never felt so long.

📋 DESCRIPTION:
Alternating movements. 0:20 seconds of work, 0:10 seconds of rest for 8 minutes total.

⟨⟩ EQUIPMENT:
Body Weight

⏱ TIME TO COMPLETE:
8 Minutes Total.

IT'S FIVE O'CLOCK SOMEWHERE

5 Minute Single leg V-Ups
5 Minute Lunges
5 Minute Plank
5 Minute Glute Bridges

Turning those saplings into sequoia trees.

📄 DESCRIPTION:

Accumulate 5 minutes total for each movement. You can mix and match any way you'd like. For example: 1 minute of each for 5 total rounds.

🏋 EQUIPMENT:
Body Weight

⏱ TIME TO COMPLETE:
For Time.

4X FLOOR

1 Inchworm
1 Push-Ups

*Inchworms move slow but gosh darn do they have a
strong cores.*

📄 DESCRIPTION:

Perform an inchworm to push-up combo starting at one end
of your room and repeat until you've reached the other end.
Complete 2 full laps.

🏋 EQUIPMENT:
Body Weight

⏱ TIME TO COMPLETE:
For Time.

SIR PLANKS A LOT

Suitcase Pull Throughs (1 per side)

Challenge yourself to sway as little as possible. Be strong like a bridge.

 **DESCRIPTION:**

In a plank position alternate pulling the suitcase from one side of your body to the other. Do this as many times as possible until you can't hold the plank. Repeat 4 more times.

 **EQUIPMENT:**

Body Weight
Suitcase

⏱ TIME TO COMPLETE:

For Time.

EMOTIONAL BAGGAGE

4 Suitcase Taps
1 Push-Up

Depending on how your day/week has gone these suitcase taps might turn into suitcase slaps. Very therapeutic.

📋 DESCRIPTION:

In a plank position put the suitcase just ahead of you at arm length distance. Touch the suitcase 4 times (2 times each hand, alternating) then perform 1 push-up. Touch the suitcase 4 more times and now do 2 Push-Ups. Continue this cycle of adding 1 push-up per round until you can no longer hold the plank position anymore.

🏋 EQUIPMENT:
Suitcase

⏱ TIME TO COMPLETE:
For Time.

RESOURCES

If you need help with any of the movements in this book or would like to see the proper form we highly recommend visiting:

www.101hotelworkouts.com

If any movements in this book are new to you, you will find all movement standards there. As always, you can sub any movement out you'd like and scale as needed. It's more important you move than it is doing these workouts to the letter.

Have a fit and free life!

Made in the USA
Las Vegas, NV
01 February 2024

85173096R00066